Magenta Style

Paper Enchantments

Magenta Style
Paper Enchantments

CREATE CHARMING CARDS, BOXES, ORNAMENTS, ALBUMS, AND MORE

NATHALIE MÉTIVIER AND LESLIE CAROLA

ST. MARTIN'S GRIFFIN

NEW YORK

www.stmartins.com

An Arena Books Associates Book
www.arenabks.com

Book concept, development, text: Leslie Carola, Arena Books Associates, LLC
Projects: Nathalie Métivier, Magenta, Inc.
Design: Elizabeth Johnsboen, Johnsboen Design
Photographs: Jon Van Gorder
Additional projects contributed by: Hélène Métivier, Marie-France Perron
Copy editor: Deborah Teipel Zindell

Thank you to Daniel Tate of Magenta for his support, and a special thank you to all the Magenta artists—Julie Adam, Valérie Dumais, Mylène Dupré, Suzanne Ouellet, and Marie-France Perron—for their constant inspiration. Thanks to BJ Berti and Jasmine Faustino; Michael Storrings and Lisa Pompilio at St. Martin's.

Library of Congress Cataloging-in-Publication Data Available Upon Request

ISBN: 978-0-312-62798-0

First Edition: May 2010

10 9 8 7 6 5 4 3 2 1

Contents

Introduction

Welcome to the enchanted world of Magenta, a heady world of color, texture, and glorious embellishments. Magenta projects are like the richest, most delectable desserts—a bit of this, a dab of that, a few of those—all pulled together into a grand surprise that delights the senses. And the bits and dabs and dollops are materials and techniques favored by paper crafters the world over.

Pleasing rhythms, a harmonious palette, and a balanced composition with a strong focal point are the basic ingredients of a good design. When creating a project, first ask yourself: what is the purpose (context) of the project, what shape and arrangement (composition) is appropriate, and are the colors harmonious? With a handful of tools, a little imagination, and a few basic techniques, you can create a varied array of effects and one-of-a-kind creative designs.

Color immediately captures our attention— glossy or matte, light or dark, intense, soft, fluid, static, lustrous, or brilliant. The effect is transformative. It is color that sets the tone in a project. Sometimes that tone is free and exotic, other times it is controlled and formal, or it may be casual, sophisticated, or even silly. The coloring might come from inked rubber-stamped images enhanced with watercolor, pigment ink, dye ink, alcohol ink, colored pencil, marker, cut colored paper, printed paper, or stickers. The inks, paints, pencils, and papers available today give you a tremendous world of color possibilities. Choosing harmonious colors is the challenge.

A color wheel is a wonderful tool to help you meet the challenge of color selection. It is a circular diagram in which primary and intermediate colors are arranged sequentially so that related colors are next to each other and complementary colors are opposite. Red, yellow, and blue are the three primary colors—the colors used to make all other colors. Orange, green, and purple are the secondary colors, made from combining two primary colors. It is intriguing to work with shades (color plus black) and tints (color plus white) of one color, with complementary colors (directly opposite colors on the color wheel), and with analogous colors (pairs of colors that are adjacent on the color wheel). Color schemes that look natural together are said to be harmonious. Harmonious elements look well together just as harmonious elements in music sound well together.

By experimenting and playing with color you will boost your own confidence and enthusiasm. Let your own creative intuition develop. Trust your own eye to tell you what does or doesn't work. You know more than you think you do. Choose your palette well. Warm (exciting) or cool (calming) colors? What color combinations please your eye? You can make a scientific decision when choosing a palette for your project, or try thinking of a favorite bouquet of flowers and select your colors from those—all or some of them. Nature's colors are rarely static.

Think of ways to use and reuse your materials. Learn to see beyond the whole shape to its individual elements. We have had fun playing with positive and negative shapes (the shape left on the sheet after the positive shape is removed), using both die-cuts and Peel Off's. And we have also used die-cut and Peel Off's shapes as templates and stencils.

Peel Off's can be the starring event or elegant accents. Fill the outline shape with alcohol ink or permanent ink markers to create a brilliant stained-glass effect or color a stamped image and cover it with a Peel Off's frame—a clear square with decorative silver edges. Or use Peel Off's flowers as a template or stencil, creating a white image on whatever color you applied over and around the design.

Magenta started as a rubber stamp company in 1992. Their lovely Canadian-made stamps immediately earned the respect of crafters worldwide. The images were beautiful; the deep-etched rubber beds produced exquisite line; and the wooden mounts and handles added a craftsman touch. Magenta hasn't strayed far from those early days, although they have added their own printed papers and embellishments to their line of art rubber stamps, often designed to accompany a particular rubber stamp.

Magenta artists are not minimalists. They love a grand production. And by observing their projects with a critical eye you can learn to create your own grand productions, Magenta style, or your own style. Perhaps multilayered and plentifully embellished, but the basic composition of a Magenta project is not complex: it is simple and balanced. Often the composition is classically centered. Or a centered composition is placed off-center on the page, adding energy and motion to the layout. Magenta artists use the term "romantic" to describe their work. And that it is. A colorful, romantic world where every detail counts. Like the finest music, Magenta projects are melodic and harmonious without being banal: they constantly surprise with their rich color, texture, and design.

A MAGENTA TIP: after mounting a Peel Off's leaf shape on decorative paper and silhouetting the image, gently scrape the back of a scissors blade against the back of the mounted image to curl it slightly—a small but telling detail. Details are everything with a Magenta project.

MAGENTA STYLE PAPER ENCHANTMENTS offers a treasure trove of ideas and inspiration. The projects lend themselves to variations. Try the projects as they are. Then try a different palette. Shift the focal point. Play with the details. That's how you'll find the art of the craft. That's the Magenta way, and we hope it will be your way. How do you start? Simply. Dig in, unleash your creativity and imagination. Celebrate the everyday moments in life. Have fun and work from your heart—Magenta Style.

Layering Color

It's a given: think of Magenta, and you think about color—luxurious color applied layer upon layer for a sumptuous burnished effect. And whether that color is applied with pencil, marker, inkpad, brush, or glittery adhesive to paper, wood, acrylic, or glass, the meticulous attention to detail is consistent.

Sophisticated Colored Pencil

Magenta artists have a reputation for using colored pencils with stunning results. A trio of cards, opposite, were all created by rubber stamping an image in black ink on a slightly "toothy" nonwhite cardstock, and adding color to the image by gently rubbing in layers of rich-toned colored pencil. Try varying the line weights and texture by changing the pressure on the colored pencil as you work. Add contrasting light and dark highlights to the edges and centers of shapes with white or dark pencil to heighten the play of light and tone, adding an unmistakable rich, luminous effect.

LIST OF MATERIALS

Card: terra cotta square, 5¼ x 5¼ inches
Cardstock: white, 3½ x 3½ inches;
  terra cotta, 3½ x 3½ inches
Stamps: Daisies Square; Daisy Post
ColorBox Ancient Page inkpad: coal black
ColorBox Cat's Eye inkpad: stucco
ColorBox Cat's Eye Fluid Chalk inkpad:
  burnt sienna
Prismacolor pencils: violet blue, violet, parma
  violet, lilac, lavender, mulberry, dark purple,
  raspberry, orange, goldenrod, white
Tools: craft knife, cutting mat, ruler,
  adhesive

Rich color effect

For a rich, dramatic result, stamp an image in dark ink on a medium-dark cardstock and color with soft, almost waxy, colored pencils.

1. Hold the stamp rubber side up in one hand and gently tap the coal black Ancient Page inkpad on the rubber image in a light circular motion. This allows you to see the application of the ink on the rubber image, and adjust the pressure and positioning of the inkpad to correct any flaws. Stamp the inked image on a terra cotta cardstock square.

2. Color the stamped image. Start building the layers of color with the darkest colors first so you can blend the colors easily and evenly overlap the previous color as necessary. Silhouette the stamped and colored image.

Tip: *Use old, slightly dry inkpads for "distressing," or lightly inking, the edges of a layered panel. If the pad is too wet, the inking will be too dominant.*

3. Stamp the Daisy Post flower in burnt sienna Fluid Chalk ink in diagonal rows across the terra cotta card leaving some image off the edge. The monochromatic palette of ink and cardstock creates a refined background focused on texture more than color. The diagonal pattern adds energy to the background.

4. Lightly brush the edges of the white card-stock square, direct-to-paper, with the stucco inkpad. Edging the white square with delicate color softens the contrast and relates the white square to both the card background and the featured stamped image. Layer the colored squares onto the stamped card.

White-Embossed Card

The loveliest cards are not necessarily the most difficult to make, but often they employ a stylish, though not obvious, element. Delicate, translucent, pearlescent inks add a distinctive touch to the delightful card, opposite. The four-square arrangement of slightly rotated blossoms offers a calm sense of order. The blossoms move around the surface of the card with each square. The outline image, stamped four times in white pigment ink on black cardstock, embossed with white embossing powder and heat set, resists the watercolor painted on top of it, leaving a lovely white border around each shape.

LIST OF MATERIALS

Card: moss green square, 5¼ x 5¼
  inches
Cardstock: black, 2½ x 8½ inches;
  ivory, 4½ x 4½ inches;
  citrus green, 4¾ x 4¾ inches
Stamp: Spring Flower
USArtQuest Watercolor Palette:
  Duo & Interference Colors—Jewelz
ColorBox Pigment inkpad: white
Embossing powder: white
Tools: heat tool, small paintbrush, cup
  of water, scissors, adhesive

Refreshing outline images

Watercolor painted over an outline image stamped in white pigment ink and embossed with white embossing powder will not stick to the embossed line. You will have an appealing raised white outline with the watercolor inside the line.

1. Stamp the Spring Flower image four times with white pigment ink on black cardstock.

2. Sprinkle white embossing powder on the wet stamped images. Set with a heat tool. When "set" the white lines will be hard and raised from the cardstock surface. If you are using a jar of embossing powder, keep a folded sheet of paper on hand to catch the excess powder and to funnel the unused powder back into the jar for future use.

Tip: Wipe the colored surface after the watercolor has dried to remove any residue of paint on the embossed white line.

3. Paint the stamped, embossed flowers with the pearlescent inks in the watercolor palette as shown, each blossom a different color. Use just a little water to brush the color evenly and keep it slightly opaque. (More water will make the painted image more translucent than we desired for this project.) Experiment to find what you prefer.

4. Layer the ivory and citrus green cardstock panels on the moss green card. Silhouette each of the four completed squares and arrange them on the matted card in a square. Here, all the blossoms are toward the center, but in the card on the previous spread, the blossoms are all to the outside of the squares. Rotate each square before adhering to the card.

Polished Surfaces

Three decorative folded boxes in varying shades of blue, white, and silver are reminiscent of graceful, earlier days. The nestled shapes, refined palette, brilliant glossy surface, and delicate size are as intriguing as they are effective. The sizes, especially the two smaller boxes, are ideal to present small gifts, grace a table as place cards, or become party favors. A mixture of two fast-drying dye-based alcohol inks made for use on slick surfaces (glossy paper, glass, acrylic, metal) were used to create the colorful patterns on the mid-sized Kromekote boxes. The box die cuts are available from Magenta—ready for coloring, folding, and embellishing.

LIST OF MATERIALS

Hexagonal box
Cardstock: Kromekote
Stamps: Swirly Branch, Bold Branch, Deco
    Flower, Sunburst Blossom
ColorBox Fluid Chalk inkpad: azurite
Adirondack Alcohol inks: sailboat blue,
  cloudy blue
Blending Solution
Peel Off's: Silver Foliage
Tools: craft sheet, scissors, adhesive,
  felt pad with handle

Sophisticated surface

The brilliant, glossy surface of Kromekote cardstock displays fast-drying, dye-based alcohol inks beautifully. The ink glides across the slippery surface.

1. Squeeze a few drops of each of two blue alcohol inks on a prepared applicator. The ink is permanent, so to prevent spills, bring the applicator up close to the tip of the ink bottle to release the ink drops. Add a few drops of Blending Solution to extend the coverage over a large surface and to help create a textured light/dark finish.

2. Place a protective sheet of paper or a craft sheet under the box before coloring to catch any excess ink. Dab the inked applicator on the front of the Kromekote box, and let it dry. Then follow the same process on the back— which will become the inside—of the box for a "finished" box interior.

3. Stamp the appropriate flower images in azurite Fluid Chalk ink in a random pattern over the colored box surface. Add coordinating Peel Off's to embellish the box. Stamp a mini flower image on the tabs at each end of the flat box and finish the smaller tabs for the top of the box with a small silver Peel Off's flower.

4. Close the box by mountain folding on all scored lines. Tuck the small tab on the right just behind the previous tab on the left side. Gently turn the box as you tuck in each tab to keep the rounded shape. The colored, folded box is a sophisticated project. Stamp and silhouette flowers to decorate the box for a more casual, country style.

Laser-Cut Image

The velvety, jewel-toned palette with light highlights emerges dramatically from the black background panel of the featured card, opposite. The white double-folded card at the right presents a quieter statement, although the shapes are also drawn and colored on a black cardstock panel but slipped between the white double-folded leaves. The long double-fold card with the laser-cut image is available as a precut card from Magenta. Use the card as a stencil and trace the design onto a black cardstock panel and then mount it on a card or use the double-folded card itself, tracing and coloring the image on black cardstock slipped between the folds.

LIST OF MATERIALS

Cards: laser-cut Flower Pot;
   white rectangular, 4¾ x 6¼ inches
Cardstock: black, 3½ x 4½ inches;
   white, 3¾ x 4¾ inches
ColorBox Cat's Eye Pigment inkpad:
   moss green
Prismacolor pencils: grass green, lime peel,
   nonphoto blue, white, lilac, pink, neon red,
   peach, chartreuse
Glossy Accents Lacquer
Tools: adhesive

Romantic color effect

Outlining with light-colored pencil helps to make soft, blended edges on the outlined shapes. Shading with evenly pressured side-to-side strokes creates a smooth layer of pigment to build on. To create shadows, increase pressure as you stroke.

1. Remove the precut pieces and store for a future project. Cut black cardstock to a 3½ x 4½-inch panel. Center the black panel behind the laser-cut image. Using the card as a stencil, trace the shapes onto the black cardstock panel with a light-colored pencil.

2. Remove and set aside the laser-cut stencil card. Draw stems and decorative centers on the traced flowers. Finish coloring with layers of colored pencil. Cut white cardstock to a 3¾ x 4¾-inch panel. Color ("distress") the edges, direct-to-paper, with the green pigment inkpad.

Tip: *Keep your colored pencils sharp. We work with a pencil sharpener close at hand for frequent freshening.*

3. Layer the two decorated panels onto the 4¾ x 6¼-inch white card.

4. Highlight the colored image with a drop or two of Glossy Accents Lacquer. The shiny surface mimics a pottery glaze on the vase and drops of dew or rain on the flower centers.

Multilayered Card

Swirls of bright Adirondack Alcohol ink in shades of purple, plum, and metallic silver create a shimmering background for this intriguing card. The featured layers literally glisten with the alcohol ink on their Kromekote surfaces. The colors are playful and brilliant. The earthy green stamped and colored square grounds the top layers and complements the lower one.

LIST OF MATERIALS

Card: white rectangular, 4¾ x 6¼ inches

Cardstock: white, 2⅜ x 2⅜ inches

Kromekote, one piece 3¾ x 4¾ inches;
  two pieces 2¼ x 2¼ inches,
  two pieces 3⁷⁄₁₆ x 4⁷⁄₁₆ inches

Decorative paper: Dancing Butterflies,
  4¼ x 5¼ inches

Cardboard tiles: two 2-inch square tiles

Stamps: Butterfly, Ornamental Swirl, Old Script

ColorBox Ancient Page inkpad: coal black

ColorBox Fluid Chalk inkpads: warm violet,
  peach pastel

Adirondack Alcohol inks: purple twilight, wild
  plum, silver, cool peri, oregano, meadow,
  mountain rose

Blending Solution

Tools: craft sheet, scissors, adhesive, paintbrush
  and palette

Metallic streaks

A high-gloss background shimmers with streaks of metallic ink—done with a flick of the wrist—and stamped images.

1. Pour the purple twilight, wild plum, and silver alcohol inks onto a nonporous surface—a craft sheet is ideal. Add a few drops of Blending Solution to help the colors mix together.

2. Place a piece of Kromekote or other heavy glossy stock glossy-side down on the ink mixture and twist the glossy stock, rubbing it in the ink to smear it with color. Add more color and Blending Solution to the mix as necessary to color a second sheet. The process is a bit messy, so color several sheets at one time to save for future use.

3. On a second piece of colored Kromekote, stamp a single butterfly with coal black Ancient Page ink. The ink dries fast on glossy paper. Pour drops of mountain rose, purple twilight, and oregano alcohol ink in a palette. Paint the stamped image with a brush. When dry, silhouette the butterfly.

4. Paint one 2¼-inch Kromekote square with purple twilight and cool peri alcohol ink, and the other with oregano and meadow green. Stamp both with the Old Script stamp and mat with white cardstock. Mat the panel colored in step 2 with white cardstock and layer on the Dancing Butterflies paper. Assemble the pieces, lifting the butterfly with mounting tape.

Colored pencils create a rich palette for nine small chipboard tiles rubber stamped with a single flower and leaves. The 3 by 3 arrangement is an effective cover for a small album. The presentation is strong and clean. The simple design, pleasing palette, and raised platforms of the tiles provide added interest.

Four small, square tiles stamped in deep brown and beige, arranged in a square on a larger square background of beige cardstock and placed off-center on a warm brown card capture our attention with a harmonious palette and attractive composition. The geometric arrangement is supported by the rectangle of type below it and complemented with the decorative soft torn border at the right.

One large rubber stamp provides a lovely framed natural scene. Stamped in dark brown ink on lightly textured apple green printed paper, the beautifully rendered image brought to life with colored pencil is an appealing gift wrap for a light-wood box. The undulating edges of the torn paper add a homespun note.

A warm palette and a symmetrical composition placed off-center are tied together with a sheer organdy ribbon. An intriguing image is stamped, colored, cut, and mounted on a white cardstock panel. The panel is adhered to the front right side of the card beside another panel, this one softly inked.

Two cards randomly stamped with the same simple rubber stamp present two substantially different palettes and effects. The choice of background color determines the basic difference in effect; the blue advances and the dark recedes.

These two cards—one with warm colors and one with cool colors—feature the same large rubber stamp of four daisy-flower panels. There is no substantial difference in the design of the cards, but the color makes all the difference. Color tells its own story.

Pale images float behind a colored background offering a rubber-stamped ghost effect. The technique is easy. Stamp the image in white pigment ink on white cardstock. When the ink dries, color the card with a ColorBox Cat's Eye inkpad. Rub off any excess ink with a dry paper towel. The lighter images peek through the dreamlike fog in a lighter shade of the applied color. Peel Off's, a brad, and a fabric flower complete the decorations.

Variations on a theme—this simple square card presents a centered composition featuring the same flower motif on three different materials. A printed vellum background supports a hand-colored canvas mat embellished with a hand-drawn design and the central stamped and colored cardstock square. The hand-drawn shapes resemble the stamped ghosted images on the elegant blue card above.

A selection of cards stamped and embossed in white and then covered with a water-color wash illustrate a variety of elegant effects.

Floral and swirl images stamped in white pigment ink, and embossed in white, resist the inks painted over them, producing the Magenta special white-outlined colored images. The background colors influence our reaction to the tags. The light background is almost ethereal, while the dark background provides a more dramatic stage for the stamped and embossed images.

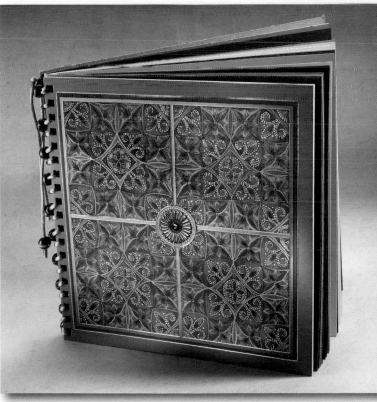

Four stamped quilt squares, shaded with colored pencils in rich autumnal colors and gold Peel Off's borders are matted and attached to an album cover. A metallic medallion painted with harmonious alcohol ink embellishes the front while a gold cord and blue beads complete the binding at the side.

A simple flower image is stamped in burgundy ink, colored with a mix of pearlescent watercolor and colored pencils. The white pearlescent watercolor "snow" is spattered on the card before embossing with clear embossing ink and clear powder.

This intriguing image is one stamp offering old-fashioned, hand-written script behind two beautiful iris flowers stamped in black and enhanced with yellow-ochre, green, and cool iris-colored pencil.

Images stamped on black cardstock, embossed in gold, and colored with pearlescent water-color inks create a dramatic, elegant presentation.

Creating Texture

Texture and dimension are magical. A rubber-stamped image colored with ink, watercolor, or colored pencils is very appealing. Emboss the stamped image and the result is stunning. Add a layer or two of mats, or a few embellishments and it is memorable. Each of these processes adds texture to a project.

Laser-Cut Shapes

Black is an elegant supportive background color. It presents the featured attraction with great style. The card, opposite, with a sophisticated palette, simple composition, and textured embellishments, makes a dramatic statement. A thin gold filament keeps our focus on the centered column of richly colored dimensional birds. The side borders, created using a Peel Off's border as a stencil, deepen the palette and add texture with the color pattern. Remember to experiment with your materials and tools to discover additional uses for them.

LIST OF MATERIALS

Card: black rectangular, 5¼ x 7¼ inches
Chipboard Birds
ColorBox Cat's Eye Pigment inkpads: amber, terra
   cotta, cyan, midnight blue
Ranger Perfect Pearls pearlescent powder:
   forever blue, blue patina, sunflower sparkle, turquoise
Peel Off's: Broad Swirls Border, Borders #2 gold,
   Border Pleasure, Hinges
Prismacolor pencils: true blue, nonphoto blue
Tools: scissors, craft knife or tweezers, adhesive, paper
   trimmer or ruler and cutting mat, craft sheet and
   scrap paper, paintbrush, Ranger Mini Mister

Chipboard art

Simple, layerable chipboard shapes provide a receptive surface and color for inks, colored pencils, and other coloring media.

1. Remove the birds and wings from a sheet of laser-cut chipboard birds. Color each bird and wing with contrasting colors of Cat's Eye Pigment inkpads. Refine the palette and texture by shading the colored birds with a light and a dark color. Color the head and back a lighter shade than the rest of the body. Experiment with your own combinations.

2. While the pigment is still wet (creamy), cover each piece with pearlescent powder by picking up a little bit of powder with a brush and spreading it lightly over the surface of each piece. Remove any excess powder with the brush. Again, you can use more than one color on the same bird for added interest.

Tip: For easy handling of small Peel Off's shapes, lift them with a tweezers.

3. Use a mini spray bottle to spritz water to "fix" the powder. When the pieces are dry, embellish the wings with colored pencil highlights and various gold Peel Off's. Attach each wing to a bird. Remove a panel the width of a Peel Off's border from the right front side of a black card, leaving the card front narrower than the back.

4. Decorate the left front edge and the inside right edge of the card with Peel Off's borders. Cover the borders with pigment ink and random touches of pearlescent powder. Remove Peel Off's to reveal the stenciled pattern. Center a thin gold Peel Off's border vertically; attach the birds, alternately facing left or right. Embellish with additional Peel Off's.

Snowflower Bouquet

This classically simple card offers an unmistakable focal point in the structured centered bouquet. The bouquet is made with silver Peel Off's flowers layered on decorative printed paper, silhouetted, and mounded one atop the other into a stunning arrangement. The layers of mounted Peel Off's textures and minimal colors create an intriguing environment: the metallic silver outlines add a shimmering luster to the cool winter palette while the canvas frame adorned with delicately hand-drawn white stars or snowflakes recedes to allow the mound of silver and blue snowflake-flowers to take centerstage.

LIST OF MATERIALS

Card: white square, 5¼ x 5¼ inches

Decorative papers: Cobalt & Tango, Ice Crystals

Canvas frame: gray self-adhesive, 4¼ x 4¼ inches

Peel Off's: silver 3D Flower

ColorBox Cat's Eye Pigment inkpads: frost white, sky blue, smoke blue, colonial blue, royal blue

Prismacolor pencil: white

Tools: scissors, 3D adhesive (mounting tape), craft knife, tweezers

Snowflower or snowflake?

It looks like a mound of snowflakes, but it's made with Peel Off's flowers. Give your imagination free reign with your materials.

1. Color directly a gray self-adhesive canvas frame with Cat's Eye Pigment inkpads. Start with dabs of the lightest color, here it's white, and add shades of blue one at a time, ending with royal blue. Overlap the edges of the ink dabs to blend the colors into a multitoned, slightly mottled surface with highlights.

2. Once the pigment ink is just, but not too, dry, draw freehand stars or snowflakes. Be sure to use a good quality, waxy, colored pencil. Avoid dry ones for this technique. Pastel crayons will also work well.

Tip: *We recommend using pigment rather than dye ink on the canvas because the canvas will absorb too much of the dye ink, making it difficult to blend the colors.*

3. Place all of the flower shapes from the sheet of Peel Off's onto two decorative papers. We have used two patterned papers—one gray and one blue. Alternate the flowers on the papers by size so that the layers of the bouquet vary. Silhouette each mounted Peel Off's flower with small scissors.

4. Mount the frame to the card. Attach small pieces of mounting tape to the back of each flower. For the very small pieces, tweezers or a craft knife are useful. Build the bouquet by layering the flowers as shown. Attach the bouquet to the card center.

Dimensional Butterfly

Teal blue and white butterfly wings seem to lift off the surface of this airy card. The patterned papers, the layered mats, and the white stamped, embossed, and colored butterfly all contribute texture to this project. The contrast of the two stamped paper squares show us that color alone can be textural. The four square panels are stamped with the same rubber stamp in white pigment ink; two are embossed in white and heat set, and the other two are colored with additional pigment inks without embossing, creating a ghosted effect. Embellishments elevate a composition, in this case literally, giving it added dimension and a little extra spice.

LIST OF MATERIALS

Card: white square, 5¼ by 5¼ inches

Cardstock: white, four 2-inch squares; 4¾-inch square; a small piece for the butterfly

Stamps: Dancing Butterflies, Butterfly

Decorative paper: Blueberry Branch

ColorBox Pigment inks: frost white, teal

ColorBox Petal Point Pigment Option Pad: Mist

Embossing powder: white

Heat tool

Summertime treasure

A light-as-air white embossed butterfly is poised over the surface of a summery card. Stamped with white pigment ink on white cardstock, embossed with white embossing powder and heat set, the added teal color is resisted by the white embossed lines.

1. Stamp the Dancing Butterflies pattern on four 2-inch white cardstock squares with white pigment ink. Emboss two of the squares with white embossing powder, and color with celadon and robin's egg Mist Petal Point petals. Wipe with a dry paper towel. Color the remaining two stamped squares with aqua and peacock pigment ink, and rub off excess ink.

2. Adhere the four inked squares on a white cardstock square, alternating the embossed and ghosted panels.

Tip: *Lift the butterfly's wings by gently holding down the body and pulling up on the wing with your fingers or a scissors blade.*

3. Center the Blueberry Branch decorative paper on a square white card, and layer the matted four stamped panels on top of the printed paper.

4. Stamp and emboss the single butterfly in white, heat set, color with peacock pigment ink, and silhouette using small scissors. Attach the butterfly to the center of the card, and gently bend the wings slightly off the surface to add some interesting dimension.

Debossed Frame

Embossing is a favorite embellishment for rubber stampers. The raised embossed image adds dimension, texture, and an enchanting note to a project. Here we are reversing the impression, so that the image is depressed into a built-up layer of clear ink (clear Top Boss) and metallic gold embossing powder. The process takes multiple layers of heat-set ink and embossing powder. An image is rubber stamped into the hot lavalike gold surface. The effect is sumptuous, especially with the contrast of the soft silk ribbon wrapped at each side. These handsome embellished corners complete the vintage frame for a sepia photograph of a lovely mother.

LIST OF MATERIALS

Cardboard frame: 7 x 7-inch outside and
  3½ x 3½-inch opening
Stamp: Architectural Pattern
Cardboard tiles: four tiles 2 x 2 inches
Top Boss inkpad: clear
ColorBox Pigment inkpad: gold
Embossing powder: gold
Peel Off's: Borders, gold
Fabric ribbon
Tools: scissors, adhesive, heat tool

Elegant, textural frame

Textural debossed gold corners and a rich silk ribbon decorate a lovely vintage frame with style.

1. Using a clear pigment such as Top Boss, cover the surface of a cardboard tile.

2. Dip the coated tile in a plate of gold embossing powder. Heat set. Repeat the clear ink, the gold powder, and the heat until the embossing becomes thick enough to receive the rubber stamped impression—probably four to five times.

Tip: Ink the rubber stamp with gold pigment ink to protect its rubber surface from the heat of the embossing, which becomes extremely hot after several coats.

3. Press firmly on the stamp, pushing it into the still-hot-almost-liquid last coat of gold embossing. The result is an image reversed, embedded in the gold instead of raised. More or less dimension is created depending on the number of coats of embossing.

4. Wrap a nice fabric ribbon several times around the four sides of the picture frame, and glue or tape the ends to the back of the frame. Glue a "debossed" tile to each corner. Embellish with strips of Peel Off's around the ribbon. Finish by coloring the sides of the tiles and frame.

Embellished Cork

Thin cork layers covered with alcohol ink are cut into pieces that fit together geometrically, like a mosaic, adding a slightly pebbled surface to a card. Panels are outlined with gold Peel Off's borders. The featured elements are gold Peel Off's birds and branches applied to the colored cork panels that have been highlighted with pearlescent watercolors. The subtle color on the cork adds intriguing depth.

LIST OF MATERIALS

Card: black rectangular, 4¾ x 6¼ inches

Cardstock: black, 4 x 5¾ inches

Decorative paper: Street Prints, 4¼ x 6 inches

Cork: 8½ x 11-inch sheet

Peel Off's: Beautiful Birds, gold

Adirondack Alcohol inks: butterscotch, stonewashed, latte, meadow, denim, pesto

USArtQuest Watercolor Palette: Pearlescent & Metallic—Jewelz

Blending Solution

Tools: ruler, craft knife, cutting mat, craft sheet, scissors, double-sided adhesive, felt pad with handle

Increased drama

A rich-toned porous base highlighted with gold Peel Off's borders offers a handsome, dramatic presentation.

1. Using a ruler, a craft knife, and a cutting mat showing measures, cut various pieces from a thin sheet of cork. Here we cut: two pieces 2½ x 2½ inches, one piece 2 x 2¾ inches, one piece 2 x 2 inches, and four pieces 1¼ x 1¼ inches. Sizes needn't be exact because you can trim the excess cork once it is mounted on the cardstock.

2. Color each of these cork pieces with the alcohol ink. Use the same felt pad for several cork panels, whether colored with one color or several combined colors. Start with the lightest tones on the pad and add darker tones.

Tip: *Color the cut cork pieces with several alcohol ink shades for increased interest.*

3. Put double-sided adhesive or any good adhesive (one that doesn't dry too fast) on the black cardstock. Cover it with the cut pieces of cork. Trim the cork flush with the cardstock.

4. Add Peel Off's borders to cover some of the junctions between pieces. Add birds and branches Peel Off's. Enhance with pearlescent watercolor to decorate the birds and branches. Mount the cork panel on the decorative paper and the black card.

Gallery

Die-cut chipboard birds colored with several shades of orange and blue inks rest on chipboard tiles covered with decorative paper brushed with ink. The project was created with a Magenta kit that supplies the chipboard materials for the framable artwork.

White cardstock is covered with rubber-stamped leafy branches in a deep red wine color and large flower shapes created using the negative shape of the chipboard flower as a template. Decorative Peel Off's, chipboard flowers, and a bird complete the design.

A chipboard album kit from Magenta offers prepunched covers plus 14 prepunched white cardstock pages ready for decorating with stamps, Peel Off's, papers, and assorted embellishments. The front cover has a die-cut window with three graphic trees in place plus assorted dimensional embellishments to position as you wish.

The strong palette of blue and burnt orange of this simpler version of the large bird card, opposite top, is modified with lighter shades enhancing the leaves, and darker shades deepening the background. The extended tones within the simple palette add drama and movement to the artwork. A small but very effective detail is the gold Peel Off's accent colored with colored pencil and lacquer on the bird's wing.

What to do when you have one chipboard flower and several cards to make? Make it a template. Templates can be used and reused to create many projects. The white flowers here were made by using a chipboard flower as a template, placing it on the blank card, and applying ink, direct-to-paper, around the dimensional flower. After inking, remove the flower to reveal the shape in white on the blue card.

A handsome card gives a simple lesson in layering stenciled images. Two different stencils and two different pink papers were used to create the pink bloom on this stylish card. Transparent Peel Off's add the smaller two shapes. Large silver Peel Off's swirls and a mini Peel Off's flower provide festive finishing touches.

Both the positive and negative laser-cut chipboard shapes are used for these cheerful, bright cards with warm palettes. Play with the colors and the shapes, and have fun.

Elegant texture and palette abound with a stunning black background supporting gold stamped and embossed leaf images colored with pearlescent watercolors.

Magical, imaginative gift wrap is not difficult. Align columns of black and white Peel Off's top and bottom on black or white cardstock and then center on a white box top. Wrap with a red satin ribbon layered with black and white fabric flowers held in place with a red brad. The tasteful wrapping is easy, effective, and fun.

A simple centered design with simple mats and a simple palette is clean and effective. One gray fabric flower and a Peel Off's embellishment, held in place with a white brad, anchors a black cardstock frame adorned with silver Peel Off's, in both positive and negative shapes.

(Above left): Torn paper, layered mats, stamped images, chipboard ornaments, and Peel Off's contribute to a charming collage.

(Above right): Multiple layers of multiple patterns in a multitude of colors sing freely of the joy of collage. Save cut pieces of paper for future use.

A mini album is covered with the same debossed pattern created for the frame on page 55. Several layers of ink and heat set embossing powder are needed to create a thick enough base in which to stamp the textural pattern.

A parade of rich, warm colors and patterns adds a homespun touch to an adapted quilt pattern, ideal as a treasure box lid or album cover. Large cardstock triangle tiles and several sizes of square tiles are stamped and colored with inks and pencils.

Designing with Peel Off's

Peel Off's—those special Magenta stickers in gold, silver, copper, white, and black—are the ideal elegant embellishment for a Magenta project. They can be colored with permanent ink markers or alcohol ink for additional decorative effects.

Coordinated Table Décor

Peel Off's come in many sizes, from tiny dots to large decorative panels. They provide color, pattern, and texture, all adding to our visual enjoyment. Simple compositions of strong, basic shapes embellished with soft, decorative sticker artwork define the suite of tabletop items, opposite. For an interesting effect, remove a one-inch panel from the right edge of the card front, decorate it, and attach it just to the left of its original position. Dab color onto the cut strip as a pleasing background for gold Peel Off's blooms adhered before attaching the strip to the card front.

LIST OF MATERIALS

For the invitation (large card in photo):

Card: white square, 5¼ x 5¼ inches

Cardstock: white square, 2¼ x 2¼ inches

Cardboard tile, 2 x 2 inches

Peel Off's: Scalloped Blooms, gold;
  Tiles, gold; Border Pleasures, gold

Sticker Borders: Classic Borders

Ranger Distress inkpad: vintage photo

USArtQuest Watercolor Palette: Pearlescent
  Stargazers

Glossy Accents Lacquer

Tools: craft knife, cutting mat, ruler,
  bone folder, scissors, adhesive,
  paintbrush, water cup, sponge pad with
  handle

Romantic invitation

Designing the invitation for a dinner party can start your creativity flowing. Develop the decorative idea you established with the handmade invitation as you create place cards, napkin rings, and small gift boxes.

1. Cut a strip with a ruler and craft knife, approximately 1 inch wide, from the right side of the card front. A metal ruler with a cork back is the easiest ruler to hold steady while cutting.

2. Color the 1-inch strip by dabbing Ranger vintage photo Distress ink on it using a sponge pad with a handle. Color the edges of a 2¼-inch cardstock square the same way but dabbing more firmly to create darker colors. Keep the center of the square clean; you will be mounting a decorated tile there. Decorate the strip with Peel Off's Scalloped Blooms.

3. Attach a Sticker Border approximately ¼ inch in from the outside border of the card interior. (Note: We find it easier to work with the card rotated 180 degrees clockwise in this step so we are not working across the folded card.) A small gold Peel Off's Border will fit in that ¼-inch space between the printed border sticker and the card edge.

4. Attach the decorated cardstock strip to the card front ¼ inch from the right edge. Add a gold Peel Off's border to its left. Attach the edged cardstock square from step 2, a 2 x 2-inch tile, and the silhouetted white cardstock square decorated with Peel Off's Scalloped Blooms painted with pearlescent watercolor. Accent flowers with Glossy Accents.

Stained-Glass Card

Glorious sunlight shining through a stained-glass window is a memorable image. Alcohol ink and Magic Tape (a wide tape designed to gather Peel Off's pieces) have allowed Magenta artists to create their own versions of stained-glass windows. The shiny tape and brilliant alcohol inks shimmer with light. Remove some of the ink daubed onto the Magic Tape with the Blending Solution to allow for spot-on accenting with various colors. By removing some of the color, any freshly applied colors will be bright and clear. Try it—though you may get lost in this magical world.

LIST OF MATERIALS

Card: white square, 5¼ x 5¼ inches

Cardstock: white, 4⅞ x 4⅞ inches; 4 x 4 inches

Decorative paper: Robin's Nest, 5 x 5 inches

Magic Tape: approximately 3 x 4 inches for the stained-glass pattern; a small piece for the flower

Peel Off's: 3D Stained Glass Flowers, gold

Adirondack Alcohol inks: meadow, pesto; butterscotch; bottle; wild plum; eggplant

Blending Solution

Tools: adhesive, scissors, craft sheet, paintbrush, palette, felt pad with handle

Colored glass effect

A glossy surface and brilliant inks create an elegant colored glass surface that simulates carefully crafted stained glass.

1. Cut a piece of Magic Tape slightly larger than the selected Peel Off's image. Color the shiny side with alcohol ink. We used a mixture of the colors meadow and pesto applied together to the felt applicator pad. Adhere the gold Peel Off's panel to the painted Magic Tape.

2. Dip a brush into a few drops of Blending Solution dropped directly on the craft sheet, and apply it to the large flower areas of the Peel Off's and any spots from which you want to remove color. You can also lighten and swirl mixed colors for added interest.

Tip: *A small piece of Magic Tape is useful for lifting small Peel Off's.*

3. Place a few drops of several colors of alcohol ink in separate wells of a clean palette. With a small brush, paint the areas from which you removed color in step 2. We used wild plum ink for the flowers. A paintbrush allows you to color small areas more precisely than the dabbed overall color applied with a felt applicator pad.

4. Place a single gold Peel Off's flower on another piece of Magic Tape, paint and silhouette it. Layer the mats. Remove the protector sheet of the Magic Tape from the decorated "window" and place the artwork off center on the mats and attach the single colored flower with mounting tape beneath it. Enhance with gold positive and negative Peel Off's leaves.

Mini Tiles Card

The warm palette, classic square shapes, and well-spaced layered mats combine to make this project appealing. Four mini tiles are stamped in Ancient Page coal black ink with two different flower images, colored with colored pencil, and covered with mini transparent Peel Off's with silver decorative borders. The tight, symmetrical, centered arrangement on multiple mats of harmonious colored decorative papers is showcased beautifully with two sets of thick and thin colorful mats. Magic Tape provides a perfect transparent glossy surface for the top, green, mat. Originally created to help transfer small leftover pieces of Peel Off's, Magic Tape is removable—easy enough to pick up; and permanent enough to stay where placed.

LIST OF MATERIALS

Tools: small acrylic block for stamps, felt pad with handle, adhesive, scissors

Card: white square, 5¼ x 5¼ inches

Cardstock: ivory, 3 x 3 inches

Decorative papers: Caribbean Odyssey,
  4¾ x 4¾ inches; Dancing Butterfly,
  4½ x 4½ inches; Robin's Nest, 3¾ x 3¾ inches

Magic Tape: 3½ x 3½-inch piece

Cardboard tiles: four 1-inch square tiles

Stamps: Floral Love cling set

ColorBox Ancient Page inkpad: coal black

Peel Off's: Clear Designer Squares
  (transparent with silver liner)

Prismacolor pencils: orange, peach, true
  blue, chartreuse, raspberry, lime peel

Adirondack Alcohol inks: meadow, stream

Four-square tiles

Four mini square tiles arranged in a tight square lifted off the surface of a card creates texture and dimension.

1. Adhere a flower image from a self-cling stamp set onto a small acrylic block. Stamp the image twice with a fast-drying black ink (Ancient Page) on ivory cardstock. Repeat with a second flower image.

2. Color each of the four stamped images with good quality, well-sharpened colored pencils. Silhouette the colored images.

3. Cover each silhouetted flower with a small (1 inch) Peel Off's silver-edged Clear Designer Square. Mount each square to a mini (1 inch) cardboard tile. With a felt applicator pad, dab a 3½-inch square of Magic Tape with two to three shades of green alcohol ink.

4. Remove the colored square of Magic Tape from its protector sheet and mount it to the 3¾-inch square of Robin's Nest decorative paper. Layer the other two decorative papers at the center of the card front in a successively smaller sequence. Finish with the mounted Magic Tape layer. Attach the four tiles to the center of the Magic Tape layer.

Rosette Stencil Card

P eel Off's are delightful embellishments in many ways. They add color, pattern, and texture to a project. But they are even more versatile than you might think. In this project we have used a Peel Off's image as a stencil, laying the Peel Off's sticker on a small white cardstock square, applying color to the cardstock direct-to-paper with ColorBox Cat's Eye Pigment inkpads over and around the Peel Off's sticker, and then removing the sticker to reveal the image preserved in white on the colored card.

LIST OF MATERIALS

Card: citrus green rectangular,
  4¾ x 6¼ inches

Cardstock: white, four pieces 2 x 2
  inches; white, 4¼ x 4¼ inches

Peel Off's: 3D rosettes (any color,
  here black)

ColorBox Cat's Eye Pigment inkpads:
  citrine, seaglass, mint, aqua, turquoise

Tools: adhesive, craft knife, ruler, cutting
  mat

Peel Off's other side

Stenciling with Peel Off's is fun and easy, and produces a pleasing effect. We used a black Peel Off's image here to make it easier to see the shape against the white cardstock.

1. Place one of the small rosettes from the Peel Off's sheet at the center of one of the 2-inch white cardstock squares. Brush the square gently right over the rosette with two colors of pigment inkpads. Experiment with the colors to find the mix you like.

2. Lift the Peel Off's to reveal the white silhouetted image. Repeat this process on a second white cardstock square. For the two remaining white squares, follow the same process using two different colors of pigment inkpads.

Tip: *Medium-sized Peel Off's make good stencils. Larger images are more difficult to handle.*

3. Color the citrus green card direct-to-paper with pigment inkpads in several shades of blue and green to obtain a gentle mottled effect. Bleed the color off the edges of the card. Pigment ink is slow drying, so if you are in a hurry avoid coloring the middle section where you will be attaching the featured panel.

4. Stencil the same rosette shape several times to create an interesting pattern on the colored areas of the card. Color in a darker tone than the background color, placing some of the stencil images off the edges of the card to add energy and motion to the design. Mount the four decorated white cardstock squares to a larger, 4¼-inch white square. Attach to the inked card.

Colorful Embellishments

Three charming, colorful boxes covered with Peel Off's—both positive and negative shapes—a simple gift tag, and a stunning decorated glass ornament create warmth and good cheer. Decorated for Christmas, winter celebrations, or any seasonal occasion, they make lovely gifts or sophisticated gift wrap for small presents. In fact, they are both gift *and* gift wrap for some lucky recipient. The outline Peel Off's shapes are colored with Ranger's Stickles Glitter Glue. These die-cut boxes are available as precut forms from Magenta. All you need to do is decorate the box and fold it on the score lines. Or you could create your own box and take inspiration from these allover patterns created with Peel Off's and Stickles Glitter Glue.

LIST OF MATERIALS

Star Box: forest green

Peel Off's: Large Flowers, gold

Magic Tape: small pieces to transfer the leftover pieces of Peel Off's

Ranger Stickles Glitter Glue: candy cane, magenta, lavender, starry night, yellow, lime green, holly

Tools: adhesive

Embellished star box

Gold Peel Off's and Stickles Glitter Glue in a variety of colors decorate a folded box with an unusual pinched top.

1. Place gold Peel Off's flowers and leaves in a random pattern over the entire surface of a forest green Star Box. Start with the outline Peel Off's pieces; they are the easiest to work with.

2. Add the leftover pieces of Peel Off's by transferring them with pieces of Magic Tape. Gather several pieces in one take, pressing the Magic Tape firmly onto the images, using your finger nails or a stylus tool. Lift the Magic Tape with Peel Off's attached, place on the box, and then press firmly and evenly before removing the Magic Tape.

Tip: It is easier to cut the large, floppy Peel Off's shapes into smaller pieces with scissors and reconstruct them on the box surface than to try to manipulate the complete image.

3. When you have finished placing the Peel Off's on the box, add color by squeezing Stickles Glitter Glue inside the outline flower shapes and at the flower centers. Let dry. It will take a while to dry, depending on the thickness of the applied Stickles.

4. Form the box by folding on the scored lines and gluing the tabs together. (We used double-sided tape.) Create the star fold on the top and bottom of the box by pinching the straight vertical lines in the center of each semicircle to make them pliable. Push in to the center on the straight fold lines, and then push gently on the four points to close the top.

Gallery

One small decorative tile in shades of peach and green on loops of a solid olive green ribbon provides a handsome wrap for a small gift. Let your imagination take flight. Design your own decorative accents.

A ribbon-bound mini album is bathed in a warm palette of deep red, orange, peach, and yellow. A deep red textured mat frames the straightforward centered composition of a gold Peel Off's floral image accented with deep rose and green Peel Off's markers. A simple, thoughtful thank you gift.

Stunning bouquets of cut decorative paper and Colors of Fall Leaves Peel Off's mounted on other decorative papers and vellum, cut, curled, and layered to create flower petal shapes are constructed in informal arrangements at the centers of these cards. A glass bead anchors the construction.

A flurry of gold and black Peel Off's shapes left over after the card at front was made adorn this handsome windowed album cover. The large flowers were transferred with Magic Tape. Pearlescent watercolor paints add color to the outline areas.

None of a Peel Off's sheet need be wasted. Here, we used the outline parts of the flowers left over from the sheet of Peel Off's used to make the album cover above. Colored pencil on black cardstock creates an intriguing palette.

A gold Peel Off's panel is layered on a piece of Magic Tape brightly colored with alcohol inks. This delightful multilayered card offers a simple process, palette, and composition. Magenta can make the simplest projects look timeless.

A similar technique to that used for the project above is offered in this refreshing card. A silver Peel Off's panel is mounted on a white cardstock square and colored with pearlescent watercolor paints. The feminine watercolor palette is extended to the layered mats and the pretty ribbon wrapped at the side.

A white gift box—a prescored Magenta "Monte Cristo" Box—and a frosted white ornament are embellished with silver-outlined transparent Peel Off's flowers and small stars. The large Peel Off's flower at the front was mounted on white cardstock and silhouetted, leaving a narrow border.

We respond immediately to color. This rather subdued palette defined by the olive green panel and dark red die-cut flower is brightened by the casual, informal materials. The combination of the palette and texture is thought-provoking.

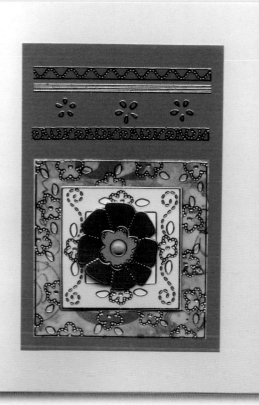

The light palette—pink, green, yellow, white, and a touch of silver outline—sings of summer and pleasant days. The three Peel Off's flowers are painted with watercolor and the torn paper edges of the panel are colored with Cat's Eye Pigment ink.

Finishing Touches

Decorative elements, in the form of Peel Off's, metal charms, additional paper, and color, can embellish many different materials ranging from chipboard to wood, glass, acrylic, and even other paper. Have fun decorating simple home objects to reflect your style in a very personal way.

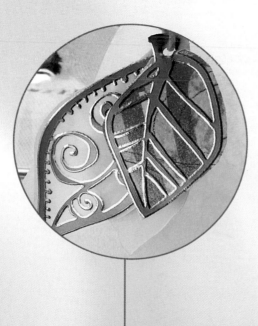

Folded Panels

Stamping and coloring are obvious Magenta specialties, but Magenta artists also have great fun with paper folding. Special folding is an engaging finishing touch to a hand-made card. A panel folded over itself provides a pocket in which to tuck another folded panel. The delicately stamped and colored card, opposite, offers a unique closing mechanism. The back of the card, already folded forward about 1¼ inches, is brought forward to slip between two stamped and colored cardstock squares attached back-to-back to the card front.

LIST OF MATERIALS

Card: white, 5¼ x 7¼ inches, landscape (or white cardstock, 5¼ x 14½ inches)

Cardstock: ivory, two pieces, 3 x 3½ inches

Decorative paper: Cherry Tree & Sepia, ¾ x 5¼ inches

Stamps: Orchid, Ornate Flourish

ColorBox Ancient Page inkpad: coal black

ColorBox Fluid Chalk inkpad: peach pastel

ColorBox Cat's Eye Pigment inkpads: olive green, amber, parchment, stucco

Prismacolor pencils: raspberry, deco orange, goldenrod, lime peel, olive green, white

Peel Off's border: Hinges

Glossy Accents Lacquer

Tools: ruler, craft knife, cutting mat, bone folder, scissors, stylus tool with white foam tips, adhesive

Folded elegance

Add dimension and hidden pockets to your cards with simple folds. The unusual closing method makes a card interesting even before it's opened.

1. Stamp the orchid image with Ancient Page coal black ink on both pieces of the ivory cardstock, color with pencils, silhouette, and set aside. Fold in half vertically a 5¼ x 14½ inch white cardstock sheet, or use a 5¼ x 7¼-inch card. Fold back 2¼ inches of the right front edge of the folded card. Press firmly with a bone folder for a firm, straight edge.

2. Fold in the right side of the card interior to barely touch the folded edge of the fold you made on the card front.

Tip: Find the grain of the paper and fold the card with the grain for a clean, flat fold.

3. Color the front of the card (except for the folded flap where it will be glued) using a stylus tool and Cat's Eye Pigment ink. (We have rotated the card 180 degrees so that the flap is not in the way as we color.) Stamp the flourish pattern two to three times with peach pastel. Color the edges of the front flap and the interior flap.

4. Adhere the decorative paper strip to the front flap. Attach the two stamped squares back-to-back on either side of the front flap, just above center. Do not put adhesive on the parts of the squares off the edge of the flap. Insert the folded interior card panel between the two stamped squares. Add Peel Off's borders and enhance flower with Glossy Accents.

Pewter Bead Necklace

Think what fun it would be to create your own necklaces to coordinate with any of your clothes or satisfy any whim. Nathalie and her sister Héléne both wear their own handmade necklaces at Magenta almost every day. Here, hand-rolled metallic beads combine with glass beads and seed beads, and with a painted-to-resemble-enamel pewter charm dangling at the front.

LIST OF MATERIALS

ChicCharm: Pewter Leaves

Metallic embellishment: Nine Botanical Tiles

Adirondack Alcohol inks: oregano, bottle

Ranger pearlescent powders: Perfect Pearls green patina, heirloom gold

Glossy Accents Lacquer

Tools: paintbrush for watercolor, palette, paintbrush for powder; scissors, skewer

To mount the necklace: Finding Kit (Tiger Tail wire, two crimps, one lobster clasp, one eyelet, three pins) and various beads: approximately 19 large glass beads, 24 small beads, and 75 seed beads); various jewel pliers

Enamel effect

Adirondack inks from Ranger are ideal for use on hard, glossy surfaces, like this metallic charm that will add a personal touch to any jewelry collection.

1. Pour a few drops of two colors of Adirondack Alcohol ink in the wells of a palette. Paint the three leaves of the charm.

2. Cover the painted leaves with Glossy Accents Lacquer. While the lacquer is still wet, sprinkle gold and green pearlescent powder over it by tapping a brush dipped into the powder over the charm. Shake off (or blow with a "whooh") the excess powder. Let the charm dry to an enamel-like finish. Drying can take several hours.

Tip: Plan ahead if you are going to paint the
metallic leaves with Glossy Accents. It can take
several hours to dry on metal.

3. To create your own metallic beads, it is easy
to use Magenta's small, soft self-adhesive
metallic embellishments tiles. Use them as
they are or paint them with alcohol ink, which
dries quickly. Use scissors to cut the width
needed and remove a small bit of the protector
sheet to expose the adhesive.

4. Roll the cut embellishment around a skewer,
starting with the protected part against the
skewer and ending with the sticky section. (If
you were to roll the sticky section first the
embellishment would be adhered to the skewer.) Create the necklace with various glass
beads and seed beads. This charm is predrilled
with three holes at the bottom edge.

Table Accessories

Try your hand at creating imaginative tabletop objects—whether for permanent or temporary display—Magenta Style. Handmade, hand-painted, and decorated home décor objects are lovely gifts, and add a personal, stylish note to festive gatherings of family and friends. The techniques are easy, the materials are inexpensive, and the process is fun. These cork-backed acrylic coasters are rubber stamped, colored with alcohol ink, and rubbed dry.

LIST OF MATERIALS

Acrylic tiles: four 3 x 3-inch

Stamp: Nine Floral Tiles

ColorBox Fluid Chalk inkpad: maroon

Adirondack Alcohol inks: red pepper, currant, butterscotch

Blending Solution

Double-sided adhesive: white sheet

Cork: 12 x 12-inch sheet

Tools: craft sheet, scissors, towels, felt pad with handle

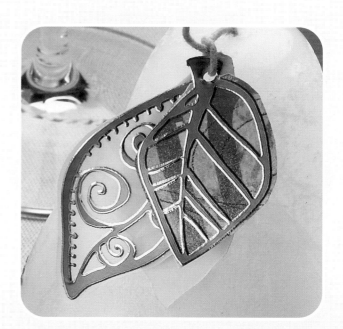

Rubber-stamped coasters

Add a refreshing touch to a party with inexpensive, handmade coasters. They make functional, personal additions to any table.

1. Squeeze drops of the selected Adirondack Alcohol inks on the felt pad. Dab the inked felt pad on the acrylic tile to cover the surface, working quickly to create a smooth base color and avoid leaving spots and marks. Let the tile dry completely.

2. Ink the stamp with a fast-drying ink, such as this maroon chalk inkpad. Center the tile, inked side down, on the inked "up" side of the rubber stamp. Press down on the tile firmly for even ink coverage. Carefully lift the tile straight up to remove it from the stamp.

3. Delicately pat the inked tile surface with a soft cloth or paper towel to dry the stamping. Finish by gently rubbing a clean soft cloth or paper towel over the tile in small circles to remove a good portion of the ink, leaving the outline of the stamp visible. Be sure the ink on the tile is completely dry.

4. Turn the tile over to attach the inked side to a piece of white double-sided adhesive. Mount the tile on a piece of cork. Trim to size with scissors.

Decorative Boxes

Have fun decorating prescored boxes of several shapes and sizes, creating your own designs and patterns with Peel Off's, pearlescent watercolor, and glitter glue. Small decorative boxes function both as gift and gift wrap. You'll find a template on page 126 for the triangular box and lid in the foreground of the photograph on the opposite page. You can enlarge or reduce the template as you wish. Create the box in several sizes, colors, and paper textures, and decorate to add dimension and festive color.

LIST OF MATERIALS

Monte Cristo Box: black
Peel Off's: 3D Clematis Flowers
Peel Off's border and dots: Border Pleasures
USArtQuest Watercolor Palette: Stargazer
  Pearlescent
Ranger Stickles Glitter Glue: starry night
Tools: craft knife or tweezers, paintbrush

Magical box

Pearlescent watercolor and gold Peel Off's create a magical embellishment for an enchanting Monte Cristo Box.

1. The interest for this box is in the off-center composition. Adhere a Peel Off's border slightly to the right of center. Add gold flower Peel Off's and leaves to create a pleasing pattern.

2. Paint the flowers and leaves with pearlescent watercolor in the watercolor palette as shown. Use just a little water to apply color evenly and to keep the colors slightly opaque. More water will make the painted image more translucent than we desired.

3. Close the box by folding (mountain folds) on the scored lines. Fold the one dotted line in the opposite direction of the other scored lines (a valley fold). There is no need for adhesive to hold the box together. The tabs and side pieces are secured under the flap of the front layers of the box.

4. Add mini drops of colorful glitter glue, like these Stickles, to the center of the flowers. Let it dry for at least 15-20 minutes.

Christmas Tree Ornaments

Glitter is fun. Think of it as whipped cream—a perfect finishing touch in one perfect dollop. Charming holiday ornaments—to decorate a Christmas tree, for display, or to give as gifts—are created by decorating plain metallic gold or opaque white glass ball ornaments with gold, copper, or silver Peel Off's and embellishing them with glitter glue and ink. The ornament in front, opposite, is finished with glitter glue applied to a Peel Off's flower—one color for each flower with a coordinated color in the center. These dazzling ornaments are not just for Christmas—use them for celebrating any occasion, from weddings to anniversaries, special birthdays to the winter solstice.

LIST OF MATERIALS

Frosted and gold ornaments

Peel Off's: 3D Clematis Flowers (for front and gold ornaments); Clear Bold Flowers with silver liner (for white/silver ornament)

Ranger Stickles Glitter Glue: starry night, lavender, magenta, lime green, holly, yellow (for front ornament)

Adirondack Alcohol ink: red pepper

Ribbon: white (for white/silver ornament)

Tools: scissors, adhesive for the ribbon

All-occasion keepsakes

A white ornament with silver and white embellishments is a study in elegance. Add some jewel-toned flowers and these shiny baubles are appropriate for any celebration.

1. Ornaments such as this one can be easily decorated with Peel Off's. We have used transparent Peel Off's delicately outlined in silver. Select the largest flower on the Peel Off's sheet and divide its petals into pairs using scissors.

2. Arrange the cut petal pairs like a necklace below the throat of the ornament. Peel Off's can be removed, if not pressed too firmly, so you can adjust the placement as you wish.

Tip: *If using Stickles Glitter Glue to color ornaments, hang the decorated ornaments to dry.*

3. Attach additional Peel Off's flowers in various sizes in a pleasing arrangement over the entire ornament surface.

4. Wrap white silk ribbon around the throat of the ornament and adhere it with a good adhesive. Add decorative ribbons through the loop.

These small square magnets were created using the same techniques as those for the coasters on page 108. Single images were stamped on a well-dried bed of alcohol ink on tiles backed with white cardstock and a magnetic sheet.

A deep wooden tray painted bright yellow is lined with a cheery multitoned pieced-quilt paper. Colorful chipboard butterflies and flowers decorate the sides.

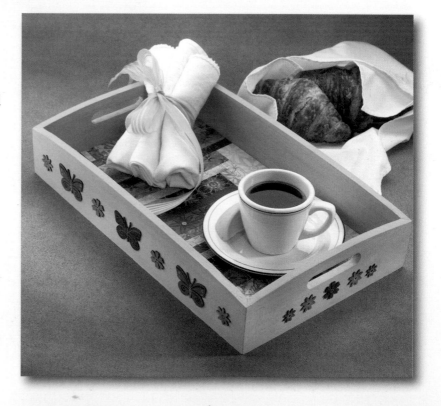

Peel Off's add a graceful note to decorated tableware. Glass and candles in subtly different shades of blue are embellished with silver Peel Off's leaves, and some are further enhanced with blue alcohol inks or Peel Off's markers. Place cards perched on stems add visual interest to the table as well as a light touch.

Pleasing palettes dominate the design constructed with Peel Off's, colorful sticker borders, and rubber-stamped, colored, and silhouetted flowers.

Three different chipboard shapes—butterfly, bird, and flower—are colored and arranged on monofilament ready to liven up any wall.

Kromekote paper provides the ideal glossy surface for alcohol inks. After the pink alcohol ink dabbed over the surface of the Kromekote is dry, a repeated pattern of a floral image is stamped in black, either in a straight or a diagonal line. Additional alcohol ink is then used to paint highlights on the flowers and leaves. The contrasting colors make a stylish presentation.

Resources

Product information for Magenta rubber stamps, Peel Off's, printed papers, metallic charms, laser-cut cards, colored pencils, and inks. These products are available through your local craft store, or contact www.magentastyle.com for information.

LAYERING COLOR

PAGES 12-13:
Rubber stamps: Daisies Square (14.372.M); Daisy Post (95.115G)
Colored pencils: Prismacolor: 933 violet blue; 932 violet; 1008 parma violet; 956 lilac; 934 lavender; 995 mulberry; 931 dark purple; 1030 raspberry; 918 orange; 1034 goldenrod; 938 white
Card: Terra Cotta square (SQC-TC)

PAGES: 16-17:
Rubber stamp: Spring Flower (14.603.I)
Watercolor: USArtQuest Palette, Duo & Interference Colors - Jewelz (PAL2).

PAGES 20-21:
Rubber stamps: Swirly Branch (14.472.H); Bold Branch (14.536.F); Deco Flower (14.193.B); Sunburst Blossom (I.0545)
Paper products: Magenta hexagonal box (PHB-K)
Peel Off's: Silver Foliage (POM3397)

PAGES 24-25:
Laser-cut card: Flower pot (CES06)
White rectangular card (CE02-R)
Colored Pencils: Prismacolor: 909 grass green; 1005 lime peel; 909 nonphoto blue; 938 white; 956 lilac; 929 pink; 1037 neon red; 939 peach; 989 chartreuse

PAGES 28-29:
Rubber stamps: Butterfly (I.0105); Ornamental Swirl (14.597.H); Old Script (24.012.J); Background (37.017.G)
White rectangular card (CE02-R)
Decorative paper: Dancing Butterflies (ME213)
Cardboard tile: 2-inch square (CT2x2)

CREATING TEXTURE

PAGES 42-43
Black rectangular card: (CE03-BK)
Die-cut: Chipboard Birds (CB608)
Peel Off's: Broad Swirls Border turquoise (POM978); Borders # 2 gold (POM834); Border Pleasures (POM3592); Hinges (POM751)

PAGES 46-47:
Peel Off's: silver 3D Flower (POM838)
Canvas frame: Grey self-adhesive (FR04-CANVAS)
Decorative paper: Cobalt & Tango (ME178); Ice Crystals (ME203)

PAGES 50-51:
Rubber stamps: Dancing Butterflies (95175.O); Butterfly (35.024.K)
Decorative paper: Blue Berry Branch (Memor 157)

PAGES 54-55:
Rubber stamp: Architectural Pattern (14.483.S)
Cardboard tiles: 2-inch square (CT2x2)
Peel Off's: Borders, gold (POM1992)

PAGES 58-59:
Black card (CE02-BK)

Decorative paper: Street Prints (ME208)
Peel Off's: Beautiful Birds, gold (POM974)
Adirondack Alcohol inks: butterscotch, stonewashed, latte, meadow, denim, pesto
Watercolor: USArtQuest Palette, Pearlescent & Metallic-Jewelz (PAL1)

DESIGNING WITH PEEL OFF'S

PAGES 72-73
White square card (SQC-R)
Cardboard Tile: 2-inch square (CT2x2)
Peel Off's: Scalloped Blooms and Tiles (POM981) Border Pleasures, gold (POM3592)
Stickers: Classic Borders (ST006)

PAGES 76-77:
Decorative paper: Robin's Nest (ME210)
Peel Off's: 3D Stained Glass Flowers, gold (POM3329)

PAGES 80-81:
Decorative paper: Robin's Nest (ME210); Dancing Butterfly (ME213); Caribbean Odyssey (ME87)
Cardboard tiles: 1-inch square (CT1x1)
Rubber stamps: Floral Love cling set (CSET11)
Peel Off's: Clear Designer Squares (POM3332)

PAGE 84-85:
Peel Off's: 3D rosettes (any color) POM3588
Citrus green rectangular card (CE02-CG)

PAGES 88-89:
Star Box: (STB-FG), forest green
Peel Off's: Large Flowers, gold (POM565)
Stickles from Ranger: candy cane (SGG01768); magenta (SGG01850); lavender (SGG01843); starry night (SGG01928); yellow (SGG01942); lime green (SGG01829); holly (SGG01812).

FINISHING TOUCHES

PAGES 100-101:
Decorative paper: Cherry Tree & Sepia (ME180)
Rubber stamps: Orchid (43.020.K); Ornate Flourish (95.182.N)
Prismacolor colored pencils: 1030 raspberry; 1010 deco orange; 1034 goldenrod; 1005 lime peel; 911 olive green; 938 white
Peel Off's: Hinges, gold (POM751)

PAGES 104-105:
ChicCharm: Pewter Leaves (CHARM021)
Metallic embellishment: Nine Botanical Tiles (E076E)

PAGES 108-109
Rubber stamp: Nine Floral Tiles (30.032.P)
Acrylic Tiles: 3-inch square (AC-03)

PAGES 112-113:
Monte-Cristo Box (MCB-BK), black
Peel Off's: 3D Clematis Flowers, gold (POM3328), Borders Pleasures, gold (POM3592)
Watercolor: USArtQuest Palette, Stargazer Pearlescent
Stickles from Ranger: Starry Night (SGG01928)

PAGES 116-117:
Peel Off's: Clear Bold Flowers (POM844)

Templates

Enlarge or reduce templates to appropriate size.
Fold on dotted lines.

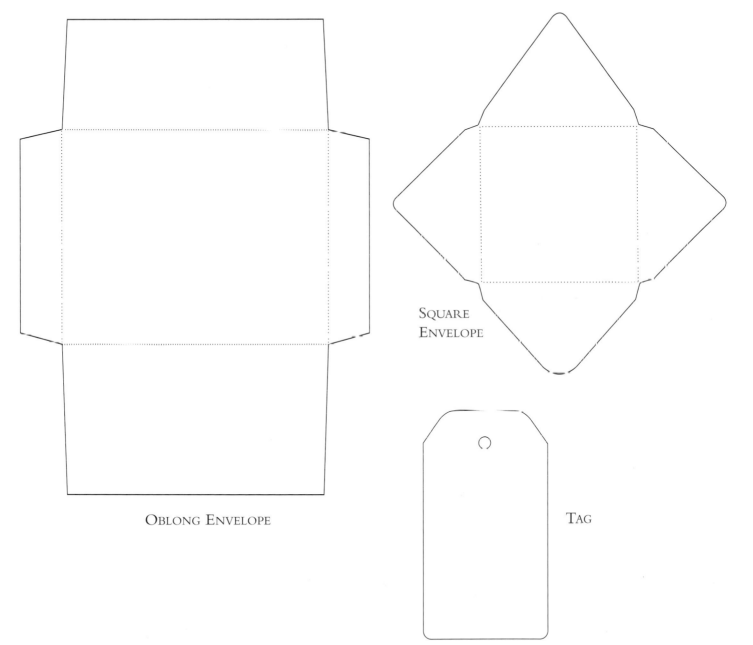

OBLONG ENVELOPE

SQUARE
ENVELOPE

TAG

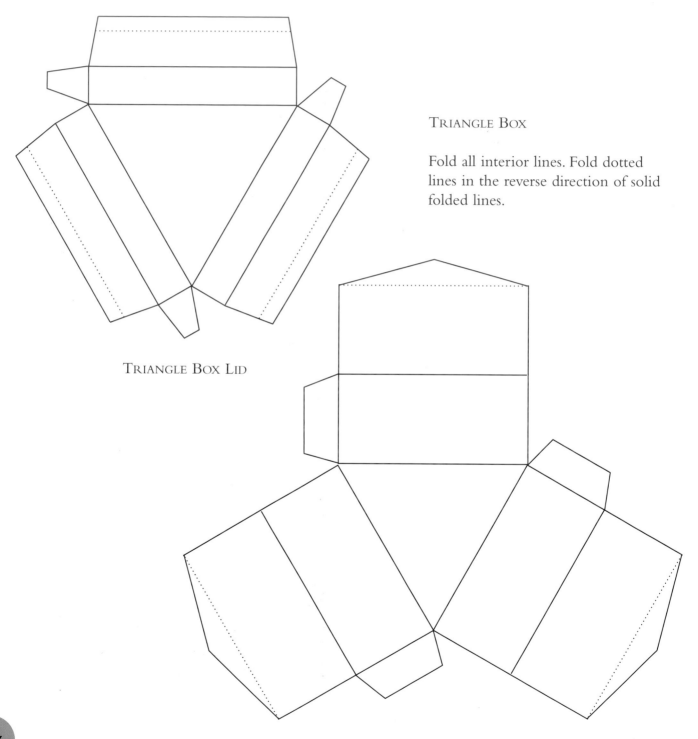

TRIANGLE BOX

Fold all interior lines. Fold dotted lines in the reverse direction of solid folded lines.

TRIANGLE BOX LID

Illustrated Glossary of Terms and Techniques

COLLAGE
Collage is a collection of artfully arranged images, papers, or other materials pasted together on a page, card, album cover, or paper-covered object. *See page 69.*

EMBOSSING
Embossing is the process of raising a rubber-stamped image on paper by applying a special powder which, when heated, rises up and becomes permanent. *See page 16.*

DEBOSSING
Debossing is a technique in which an image is rubber stamped into a multilayered surface of pigment ink. The image is depressed into the surface rather than raised as in an embossed image. *See page 54.*

FAUX ENAMEL FINISH
A faux enamel finish is acquired by adding small dollops of glistening clear lacquer to inked images. *See page 100.*

DIE-CUTS
Die-cuts are cut paper, chipboard, or shapes of other materials, similar to stickers but without the adhesive backing, suitable to attach to craft projects. *See page 42.*

GEOMETRY
Simple geometric shapes like squares, rectangles, and triangles lend themselves easily to handsome compositions with cleanly cut shapes fitting next to each other. *See page 80.*

DIMENSIONAL GLAZE
Dimensional glaze is a water-based decorative adhesive to apply directly over artwork for a raised lacquer-like finish. The glaze can be clear or colored; some variations—like Stickles—contain glitter. *See page 116.*

PAPER FOLDING
With just a few carefully placed folds, you can create imaginative three-dimensional shapes of all levels of complexity. *See page 112.*

DIRECT-TO-PAPER INKING TECHNIQUE
Direct-to-paper is a technique of applying ink onto paper with an ink pad, Cat's Eyes, or dauber. Pigment inks work best because they can be blended before they dry. *See page 33.*

PAPER LAYERING
Paper layering can mean silhouetting an object and placing it on a design; placing light paper, like vellum, over an image to screen or soften the image; or framing an image by placing multiple papers behind it. *See page 28.*

PAPER QUILTING
Quilt designs can be adapted to create stunning borders, frames, or even the central motif of a card or other craft project. *See page 68 top.*

STAMPING, "GHOST"
"Ghost" stamping is a technique that allows pale images that have been stamped in white pigment ink to peek through the haze of color applied direct-to-paper over them. *See page 35 top.*

PEEL OFF'S
Peel Off's are Magenta's special stickers, available in several finishes. You can add color to the Peel Off's with various techniques for increased effect. *See page 88.*

STENCIL
A stencil is a pattern or design cut from a material through which a substance like ink or paint is forced onto a surface. It is the negative shape left after a positive shape is removed. *See page 24.*

PEWTER BEADS
Pewter beads for use in necklaces or bracelets are made by rolling narrow strips of pewter paper with an adhesive backing around skewers. Embossed paper adds texture and heft when rolling the bead on the skewer. *See page 104.*

TEMPLATE
A template is a design or pattern used to create a shape. Unlike a stencil, where you trace the inside of a shape, a template is the shape itself, and you trace around its outside edge. You can use both forms in your artwork. *See page 65.*

RUBBER STAMPING
Rubber stamping is the technique of creating a design by tapping an inked rubber stamp on paper. The supplies you need for stamping are few: stamps, ink, paper. The embellishing supplies available are many. *See page 12.*

THREE-DIMENSIONAL CONSTRUCTION
A three-dimensional construction consists of many layers of silhouetted components built up to form a pleasing arrangement. *See page 46.*

STAINED-GLASS WINDOW PANEL
A stained-glass window effect can be created with Peel Off's, alcohol ink, and permanent ink markers. Lift the Peel Off's from their backing sheet, place them on an acetate sheet, and add color inside the outline shape. *See page 76.*

TORN PAPER
Paper itself is an extraordinarily versatile embellishment. And the soft, undulating edge of torn paper adds grace, color, and dimension. *See page 33 top.*